STOP.
YAY!

STOP.

COMMANDS THE FULL STOP

BY ROB LISLE

First Published 2026 by
Redback Publishing
Suite 6, 13a Narabang Way,
Belrose NSW 2085
Australia

www.redbackpublishing.com
orders@redbackpublishing.com

ISBN 978-1-761402-13-5

Author: Rob Lisle
Editor: Simone Saba
Designer: Redback Publishing
Illustrator: Rob Lisle

Originated by Redback Publishing

A catalogue record for this book is available from the National Library of Australia

STOP.

COMMANDS THE FULL STOP

A sentence can't really be a sentence without a full stop.

You got it, Captain Moustache.
Roggo Doggo and I know just who to recruit.
Sounds like one sick puppy.
TAP TAP

A full stop marks the end of a sentence that makes a **statement**, not a question or exclamation.

You're not getting out of here alive, heroes.
Good to see you, Rodger Dodger.
Steve-32, you might want to hurry.
Don't just stand there, Steves. Get him.
CAUTION CROCODILES
Almost done.
Good, because it's nearly lunch time.
I heard someone say lunch.

A full stop signifies the end of a **complete thought** or **idea**.

I've never been good at mazes.
Ah rats, no sign of Super Susan yet.
I should have called in sick today.
Oi, you can't just leave that here.
Something smells poopy.
SNIFF SNIFF
That's not cheese.
Hmm, clearly I went the wrong way.
Super Susan, I think we're lost.

Put a **single space** after a full stop. Then begin the next sentence with a **capital letter**.

Um, yes. Any minute now my mouse friend will break open my capsule. Then we can make our daring escape.
Red and blue wires are done. Next is either green or yellow. I think it's yellow.
I wish I had a mouse friend. We could play hide and squeak.
I'll be your friend, Goggles. We can chase tennis balls together.

Full stops are also used at the end of **imperative sentences** such as **commands** or sentences that give **instruction**.

You're going to have to wait. I've got more balancing to do.
Take it nice and easy, Punk Ninja.
Stand still. I'll catch you.
Don't stain my delicates.
Robo-Ball, you'll have to fly under his butt and let him sit on you.
Wait till I'm dry before getting me down.
Surrender to the Steves, heroes.

Use a full stop after **abbreviations** where the last letter of the abbreviation is not the same as the last letter of the full word.

I flew in from the U.S.A. to party with you.
I could dance from a.m. to p.m. every day.
I'm so good at this I might need a new name, e.g. Prof. Party Paws!
I could teach you approx. ten dances, like the boogie, the waltz, the foxtrot, etc.

When making a **list**, a full stop is used at the **end** of a full sentence.

I can tell you my three *least* favourite things:
• Uninvited guests
• Emergencies
• Shoes on my couches
THINGS TO REMEMBER
• When listing items in a sentence separated by commas, do not use full stops between items.
• In numbered or bulleted lists where each item is a full sentence, use full stops at the end.
• If the list items are phrases, omit full stops.
• Bleep
• Bloop
• Blurp
1. I like mice with soft fur.
2. Fizzy drinks - but in cans, not bottles.
3. I love Big Blue's comfy couches.
Guys, that's so much to remember. I need to write it down.
• Food
• Tennis balls
• Dancing

Without a full stop a sentence can go on and on and on.
The gang's all here now, folks, so Dr. Squid is in real trouble, but it's important you stay hydrated and keep an eye on your team mates, then we'll get ice cream later, and watch cartoons–
Blah, blah, blah.
Drink lots of water. Got it.
I heard something about ice cream.

When we find Dr. Squid I need you all to forget about how sweaty and stinky you are and focus on defeating him by dodging his tentacles and bop him with all your power before he's able to grab you and–
Dodge his tentacles. Got it.
Bop him with all our power. Got it.
Forget how stinky everyone is. I'll try.
Too many words, not enough breaks.

Full stops are also used to end **indirect questions**.

If you ask me, it's time to boost the power.
I'm not sure if our shooty-beams are working properly.
Grr. Grrrr. Grr.
My new mouse friend wants to know if we're going to win or not.
I can't tell if this is helping.

Good punctuation is important and it all starts with a stop - a **full stop**.

"A hero is brave, kind and on time."
Capt. Moustache
MORE THINGS TO REMEMBER
When a sentence within quotation marks is a complete sentence, the full stop goes inside the closing quotation mark.
I always knew we were going to win.
Still looking good.
I told you I had him.
Hi Mum.
I'm ready for ice cream and cartoons now.

Full stops help the reader take a little **break**.

The break is over. There's more to do. Let's go.

Now that you're a FULL STOP master, use your new skills to let us know what these mice are doing.

Flip back through the book to find these scenes.

ACTIVITIES

STOP RIGHT THERE!

OBJECTIVE	Identify where full stops belong in spoken language.
STEPS	• Read an unpunctuated sentence aloud with no pauses. • Ask kids: "Did that sound right?" • Re-read the sentence with full stops, pausing at each one. • Discuss the difference.
EXAMPLE	I do we have to wait Gorilla Cowboy will break us out I do. We have to wait, Gorilla Cowboy will break us out.
BONUS ACTIVITY	Have children clap, sit or freeze when they hear a full stop.

STOP AND SKETCH

OBJECTIVE	Match full stops with meaning and sentence completion.
STEPS	• Give children a sentence with a full stop. • Ask them to draw what's happening in the sentence. • Discuss how the full stop shows a full idea.
EXAMPLE	Punk Ninja is walking on the clothes line.
BONUS ACTIVITY	Let children write and illustrate their own one-sentence story.

NARRATIVE TEXT

Rodger Dodger has been gathering a group of powerful heroes in his search for Super Susan and Robo-Ball Rodger Dodger Roggo Dogg and Goggles find themselves crawling through vents there are many Steves following after them and trying to stop them the vents are a maze and the heroes find themselves lost one of the Steves waits sneakily for Roggo Doggo who has left his own little trap in the vents luckily Super Susan has not yet been caught let's hope Rodger Dodger finds her before the Steves do

THE FULL STOP FIXER

OBJECTIVE	Practise editing sentences by adding full stops.
STEPS	• Have the kids read the provided narrative based on a spread from the book. Notice the lack of punctuation. • Let them become 'Full Stop Fixers' by rewriting the text with correct punctuation.
BONUS ACTIVITY	Give them red pens or stickers to mark their fixes like real editors.

EXAMPLE

Rodger Dodger has been gathering a group of powerful heroes

Rodger Dodger has been gathering a group of powerful heroes.

SENTENCE BUILDING BLOCKS

OBJECTIVE

Understand how full stops separate ideas.

STEPS

- Write parts of different sentences on blocks or cards.
- Mix them up.
- Children build complete sentences and place a full stop at the end.

EXAMPLES

Rodger Doger

took the crew

to the disco

it was

loud

BONUS ACTIVITY

Let them colour-code sentence parts and punctuation marks.

BUILD A STORY – ONE STOP AT A TIME

OBJECTIVE

Create a collaborative story with clearly marked full stops.

STEPS

- Using the characters of the book, the kids sit in groups and take turns adding one sentence to a story.
- Each kid must finish their story with a full stop before the next begins.

EXAMPLES

Child 1:
Rodger Dodger has lost his cape.

Child 2:
He called Roggo Doggo to help him find it.

BONUS ACTIVITY

Turn it into a comic strip with one sentence and full stop per panel.

DOT TALK

OBJECTIVE	Speak in full-stop sentences only!
STEPS	• Put children into pairs and have them describe Rodger Dodger's adventure. • Every time they say a sentence, have them stop completely at the end. They are not to join their next sentence with 'and'!
BONUS ACTIVITY	Play 'Spot the Run-On', and if someone forgets a full stop, buzz them!

EXAMPLE

There is a villain called Dr. Squid. Rodger Dodger has to stop him. He needs to find help first.

DOT IT WITH DICE

OBJECTIVE	Roll the dice and write that many full-stop sentences.
STEPS	• Provide children with a die (or have them draw a number) • Have them pick a spread from the book and describe what is happening with as many sentences as they rolled on the dice.
BONUS ACTIVITY	Make all your sentences about one funny topic!

EXAMPLE

The team goes to find Punk Ninja. He is in the middle of balancing.

COLLECT ALL THE BOOKS
IN THE **PUNCTUATION EXPEDITION** SERIES!

WAIT,
HUH?